ENTREPRENEURIAL SUCCESS SECRETS:

Strategies to Start and Grow Your Business

Copyright Contents

TABLE OF CONTENT

Chapter 1: The Entrepreneurial Mindset

Entrepreneurship is a fantastic adventure, full of obstacles, possibilities, and the possibility of amazing success. The attitude of the people who begin on this journey defines the entrepreneurial experience at its heart. In this first chapter, we will look at the fundamental concepts of entrepreneurship and the critical role that mentality plays in obtaining success. We will look at the features, behaviors, and attitudes that identify successful entrepreneurs and give practical advice on how to create the correct mentality for your entrepreneurial journey.

The Influence of Mindset

Before we get into the fundamentals of entrepreneurship, let's first appreciate the importance of mentality. The mentality is the lens through which we interpret our experiences and see the world. It includes our ideas, attitudes, and mental processes, all of which have a significant impact on our behaviors and choices.

The appropriate mentality might be the difference between flourishing and just surviving in the setting of business. Successful entrepreneurs are distinguished by a mentality that drives them ahead even in the face of adversity, not only by their commercial acumen or industry expertise. To demonstrate this idea, consider the fundamental elements of an entrepreneurial attitude.

Successful Entrepreneurs' Personalities

Visionary Thinking: Successful business owners have visionary thinking. They have a distinct sense of purpose and can picture the future they wish to build. This goal becomes their North Star, leading them through the business's complexity.

Entrepreneurship is dangerous by nature, and successful entrepreneurs accept this risk. They have the confidence to take measured chances, recognizing that failure is a positive learning experience rather than a setback.

Resilience: The business road is fraught with ups and downs, and failure is unavoidable. Failures are used as stepping stones to future success by resilient entrepreneurs.

Flexibility: The business environment is ever-changing, and flexibility is essential. In reaction to changing market circumstances, successful entrepreneurs may pivot, shift direction, and adapt their tactics.

Passion and persistence: An entrepreneur's drive is fuelled by passion, while persistence keeps them going. Their dedication to their vision and strong conviction in their objectives are characteristics of their success.

Entrepreneurial success often arises from the capacity to think creatively and innovate. Successful entrepreneurs are always looking for new ways to solve old issues.

Building Networks: No one succeeds in solitude. Successful entrepreneurs cultivate a strong network of mentors, advisers, and like-minded people. They recognize the importance of teamwork and actively seek out chances to learn from others.

Developing an Entrepreneurial Mindset

Now that we've discovered the key qualities of great entrepreneurs, the issue is whether you can nurture and grow this attitude. Yes, it is a resounding yes. While some people are born with these characteristics, the entrepreneurial mentality may be developed and enhanced through deliberate effort and self-awareness.

Here are some practical tips and tactics to help you develop the correct entrepreneurial mindset:

1. Self-awareness: Begin by recognizing your own strengths and flaws. The entrepreneurial mentality is founded on a foundation of self-awareness. Determine your fundamental values, interests, and passions. The

7

first step in aligning your attitude with your business objectives is to understand what genuinely motivates you.

2. Goal Setting: Establish defined, measurable objectives. Your vision should be backed with measurable and trackable goals. This not only offers you a feeling of direction but also a blueprint for your business path.

3. Positive Self-Talk: Identify and change negative thinking habits. Your inner conversation has a huge impact on your thinking. Self-doubt should be replaced with self-belief and self-criticism with self-encouragement. A positive self-talk strategy might help you stay motivated and determined.

4. Lifelong Learning: Successful entrepreneurs are lifelong students. Make a continuing commitment to education and skill development. This may be accomplished via formal education, mentoring, or self-study. Keep up to date on industry developments and market movements.

5. Accept Failure: Change your attitude about failure. Instead of seeing it as a hindrance, consider it a stepping stone to success. Each failure teaches you something that will help you get closer to your objectives. Allow your fear of failure to inspire you rather than immobilize you.

6. Resilience Training: Practice mindfulness, meditation, or other stress-reduction practices to strengthen your resilience. Resilience is about more than just overcoming hardship; it is also about sustaining your well-being throughout difficult times.

7. Networking and Mentoring: Surround yourself with others who share your vision and enthusiasm. Look for mentors and advisers who may provide advice and assistance. A strong network may help you get insights, open doors, and negotiate the intricacies of business.

8. Visualization: Use visualization methods to clearly visualize your accomplishment and achievement of your objectives. This might serve to strengthen your dedication to your goal and drive through difficult times.

9. Adaptability: Create an attitude that welcomes change. Be receptive to comments, changes in the market, and new possibilities. Adaptability is a key attribute in the business sector.

10. Work-Life Balance: Work-life balance is really important. Entrepreneurship might be stressful, but it is critical to preserve your physical and emotional health. Even the most robust thinking may be eroded by burnout.

Finally, the entrepreneurial attitude serves as the cornerstone of company success. It describes how you approach problems, opportunities, and decisions. While some people are born with these characteristics, the entrepreneurial mentality can be grown and developed vthroughself-awareness, intentionality, and ongoing progress. You may create the framework for a successful entrepreneurial journey by adopting visionary thinking, risk-taking, resilience, flexibility, and a dedication to innovation. As you read on, we'll dig further into the complexities of entrepreneurship, building on the ideas presented in this first chapter to provide you with the strategies and resources you need to start and expand your firm.

Chapter 2: Finding Your Passion and Purpose

To build a successful business, you must first identify your true passion and purpose. Chapter 2 is all about self-discovery and introspection. We guide you through the process of finding what truly drives you and how to align your business goals with your personal values, ensuring your entrepreneurial venture is not just profitable but also fulfilling.

Success in the area of entrepreneurship, where ambition and invention collide, often depends on the connection of one's own passion with a larger purpose. The pathway to developing a great company starts with an understanding of one's deepest goals and a dedication to a strong sense of purpose. The second chapter, fittingly named "Finding Your Passion and Purpose," is a must-read for anybody interested in self-discovery and introspection. In the next 5,000 words, we will go on a deep dive into how you may determine what actually motivates you and align your company objectives with your personal beliefs, guaranteeing that your entrepreneurial endeavor is not just successful but also profoundly gratifying

The Search for Meaning and Passion

Before getting into the practical tactics for defining your passion and purpose, consider why this quest is critical to business success. Your passion feeds your entrepreneurial energy, while your purpose serves as a compass, directing you toward meaningful and significant company ventures. They form a potent mix that may drive you past the hurdles of business.

The concept that a company that connects with your passion and purpose is more likely to thrive is at the center of this journey. When you actually like what you do, it becomes more than a means to an end. It transforms into a vocation, a chance to make a difference, and a source of long-term inspiration.

Determining Passion

Passion is defined as an extreme excitement, zeal, or profound interest in anything. It is the spark that piques your interest and motivates you to pursue certain activities, hobbies, or areas of interest. When you are enthusiastic about something, you are more likely to devote your time and energy to it.

Passion may present itself in a variety of ways for businesses. It might be a passion for a certain sector, an unflinching dedication to addressing a specific issue, or a drive to deliver a one-of-a-kind product or service to the world. Your passion is the source of your creativity and tenacity, making it a crucial component of your business path.

Understanding the Goal

Purpose, on the other hand, is the motivation for your activities. The "why" drives you ahead, surpassing simple self-interest. Purpose adds meaning to your life and work by linking your activities with your beliefs and creating a greater feeling of duty.

In the entrepreneurial setting, purpose is often associated with the positive influence you want to achieve via your firm. Your goal might be to solve a social issue, enhance people's lives, or contribute to a more sustainable and equitable future. Finding your mission may help your company become a force for good, motivating both you and your stakeholders.

The Meeting of Passion and Purpose

Entrepreneurs thrive at the intersection of passion and purpose. It is the point at which your interests and values coincide, enabling you to establish a company that is both successful and personally gratifying. This alignment may lead to greater creativity, drive, and resilience, which are all essential for business success.

Consider a company in which every problem you confront, every choice you make, and every effort you make is in line with your deepest aspirations and devotion to a larger good. A company like this is more than just a source of cash; it's also a source of inspiration, reflecting who you are and what you stand for.

The Self-Discovery Process

Finding your passion and purpose is a dynamic and continuing process, not a one-time event. It requires self-awareness, introspection, and a desire to delve into the depths of one's existence. Let's break down the process into concrete stages to assist you in getting started on your trip.

1. Consider Your Interests

Make a list of things that actually fascinate and thrill you. What subjects, hobbies, or causes pique your interest? Personal and professional interests may coexist. They might be interests, societal concerns, or professional domains. Spend some time brainstorming and writing down anything that comes to mind.

2. Recognize Your Strengths and Talents

Your innate skills and talents often coincide with your interests. What do you excel at? What do people praise you for? Determine your particular abilities and skills. Sometimes your passion might be found in the things you succeed at.

3. Consider Your Values

The moral and ethical ideals that govern your life are your values. What is it that you actually believe in? What are your non-negotiable principles? Your values are critical in determining your mission.

4. Express Your Emotions

Take note of your emotional reactions. What activities or causes elicit strong feelings in you? What makes you happy, excited, or even enraged? Emotions may be potent indications of what is most important to you.

5. Investigate Your Past

Consider your life experiences. What events or accomplishments have given you the greatest satisfaction? In contrast, what encounters have left you feeling unsatisfied? Your history might provide useful insights into your interests and goals.

6. Look for Inspiration

Gather ideas from others. Read books, listen to podcasts, or watch films about people who have discovered their calling. Their experiences might give useful insights and motivation for your own journey.

7. Try new things and take action

You may not always uncover your passion and purpose via introspection. You may need to try new things, volunteer for issues you care about, or start modest initiatives. Action often leads to insight.

8. Request Feedback

Share your ideas and opinions with friends, family, and mentors. They may provide useful feedback and diverse points of view that can help you acquire a better understanding of your interests and purpose.

9. Identify Your Special Contribution

Think about how your passion and purpose may be translated into a one-of-a-kind gift to the world. What unique and important services can you provide? This is the core of becoming an entrepreneur.

Entrepreneurs Who Discovered Their Passion and Purpose in Case Studies

Let's look at two amazing case studies to demonstrate the process of discovering passion and purpose in the business world:

Elon Musk, CEO of SpaceX and Tesla, is the first case study.

Elon Musk is well-known for his interest in space exploration and sustainability. He started SpaceX with the purpose of lowering the cost of space travel and, eventually, making life multi-planetary. His love of space, along with a desire to ensure humanity's existence, has motivated him to do extraordinary deeds.

Case Study 2: TOMS Shoes Founder Blake Mycoskie

Blake Mycoskie's love of travel and adventure prompted him to learn about the significance of footwear in many poor nations. This insight motivated him to create TOMS, a firm that donates a pair of shoes to a kid in need for every pair sold. He turned a love of adventure into a mission-driven company that has had a huge beneficial effect.

Entrepreneurial Success Through Alignment

After you've found your passion and purpose, the next step is to connect them to your company objectives.

Aligning your own beliefs and goals with those of your company may be a tremendous stimulus for success.

1. Establish Your Company's Mission and Values

Your company's mission statement should represent your objective. It should clearly reflect the good influence you want to have. Establish a set of basic principles to which your company will adhere. These ideals should align with your own convictions and influence corporate decision-making.

2. Select the Appropriate Industry or Niche

If your passion is to solve a specific social problem, make sure your company works in an industry or specialty that is relevant to that issue. Consider creating a company in renewable energy, eco-friendly goods, or conservation if you are enthusiastic about environmental sustainability.

3. Determine Your Unique Selling Proposition (USP).

Your passion may become your unique selling point. Highlight what distinguishes your company and how your passion influences the quality, originality, or effect of your goods or services. Customers who share your beliefs may find your enthusiasm to be an engaging selling element.

4. Put Together a Team that Shares Your Values

Choose team members and collaborators who share your passion and mission. A team that shares your vision may help to create a good work environment and strengthen your company's alignment with its basic principles.

5. Maintain Your Commitment

Maintaining congruence between your passion, purpose, and company objectives takes dedication. Maintain your ideals even when presented with difficult options. Your steadfast dedication may motivate others and build trust with your customers and stakeholders.

Success Stories: Companies Fueled by Passion and Purpose

Let's look at two success stories of firms that were inspired by their founders' passion and purpose:

Patagonia is the first success story.

Yvon Chouinard created Patagonia, an outdoor apparel and gear brand. His love of climbing and the outdoors led to a strong dedication to environmental sustainability. Patagonia's mission statement is "We're in business to save our home planet," demonstrating their commitment to environmental stewardship. Their purpose-driven approach has garnered them not just a devoted consumer base but has also assisted them in pioneering sustainable methods in the garment business.

Success Story Number Two: Warby Parker

Warby Parker, a well-known eyeglasses firm, was formed by four friends who had a desire to make cheap, fashionable eyewear available to everyone. Their goal was to solve the market's scarcity of low-cost eyeglasses. Warby Parker provides a pair of spectacles to someone in need for every pair sold. Customers have responded positively to this purpose-driven company approach, which has contributed to their success.

Measuring Success Aside from Profit

While financial success is unquestionably vital for every organization, it is also critical to assess success in non-monetary terms. Businesses that are in line with the founder's passion and purpose often find satisfaction in a variety of ways:

Influence on Society: Businesses that are motivated by passion and purpose frequently have a good influence on society. These companies help to make the world a better place, whether via creative solutions, social responsibility, or community involvement.

Customer Loyalty: Customers who share your beliefs are more likely to become brand loyalists. They value the fact that your company stands for something other than profit.

Employee Satisfaction: A mission-driven company can recruit and retain individuals who are enthusiastic about your cause. As a result, employees will be more engaged and driven.

Personal Fulfillment: This is maybe the most crucial reward. Knowing that your company is in line with your passion and purpose may provide a profound feeling of fulfillment and joy.

Real-World Methods for Juggling Passion and Profi

While discovering your passion and purpose is an important first step, maintaining a balance between these personal convictions and financial success may be difficult. Here are some tips to help you manage this tricky balance:

Establish Clear limits: Define your corporate objectives and personal principles clearly, and set limits to avoid one from overshadowing the other. This insight will help you make decisions.

Monitor and Adjust: Constantly examine your business's alignment with your passion and mission. Be prepared to make appropriate modifications if you find misalignment.

Keep Your Stakeholders Informed: Keep your staff, investors, and consumers up to date on your passion and mission. Encourage open communication and feedback so that everyone feels invested in advancing your objective.

Measure influence: Create measurements to assess your company's influence on your chosen cause or goal. Keep track of and convey the impact your company is having.

Stay Flexible: The entrepreneurial world is ever-changing. Be prepared to modify your strategy to changing situations while adhering to your basic ideals.

The Way Forward

There is no one-size-fits-all approach to success in the world of business. However, aligning your passion and purpose with your company objectives will dramatically boost your chances of obtaining not just financial success but also profound personal satisfaction in your entrepreneurial path.

This chapter has walked you through the phases of self-discovery and identifying your passion and purpose. It has shown the transforming impact of integrating your personal principles into your commercial operations. As you go through "Entrepreneurial Success Secrets: Strategies to Start and Grow Your Business," bear in mind that passion and purpose may be your most powerful friends, driving you toward a business that is not just profitable but also profoundly meaningful.

Chapter 3: Getting Through the Startup Phase

The entrepreneurial journey is fraught with both thrilling opportunities and difficult hurdles. The launch period, typically regarded as the first obstacle, is a vital crossroads that may define the course of your organization. This chapter, appropriately named "Navigating the Startup Phase," will delve into the complexities of converting your company concept become a reality. We will cover important issues including business planning, financing choices, and laying a solid foundation for your firm. By the conclusion of this in-depth talk, you'll be better prepared to put your company on the route to development and success.

The Importance of the Startup Stage

The startup phase serves as the basis for your business goals. It's when ideas become actions, passion meets practicality, and your vision starts to take form in the actual world. While it might be tough and unpredictable, it is also a time of great possibility and enthusiasm.

In essence, the startup period involves the birth of a vision, a brand, and a legacy, as well as the birth of a firm. Here are some of the reasons why this stage is so important:

1. Concept Validation: During this phase, you validate your company concept to see whether or not it has the potential to become a successful, profitable enterprise.

2. Initial Impressions: Your company's initial impressions are formed during the startup period. The way you manage this stage might have an impact on your reputation and brand impression.

3. Learning and Adaptation: The startup phase is an experience in learning. You'll learn about your market, your competitors, and your strengths, allowing you to adjust and flourish.

4. Financial Foundations: This is where you lay the groundwork for your company's finances. The way you handle your resources during this time will have a substantial influence on your future financial security.

5. Goal setting is the process of defining your short-term and long-term objectives, as well as methods for achieving them. Your attitude during the initial period might set the tone for the next years.

6. Building a squad: If you haven't already, you'll start assembling your squad. The people you bring on board at this period will be critical to your journey

Now, let's look at the important components of successfully navigating the startup period.

Business Planning: The Roadmap to Success

Comprehensive business planning is one of the core foundations of a successful company. Consider a business plan to be the roadmap for your new enterprise. It describes your objectives, plans, and the measures you'll take to make your vision a reality.

Why Do You Need a Business Plan?

A well-structured company strategy serves numerous important functions:

Clarity and Focus: It clarifies your company's idea and goals. It pushes you to think thoroughly about your company while remaining focused.

A business plan is an important tool for communicating your vision to stakeholders, whether they be possible investors, partners, or team members.

It provides a blueprint for your company journey, describing your short-term and long-term objectives, strategies, and timetable for accomplishing them.

A business plan assists in risk management by doing a comprehensive study and identifying possible obstacles.

Resource Allocation: It assists you in successfully allocating resources and understanding the financial repercussions of your actions.

Measuring success: Using a business plan, you may measure your success against your original objectives and adjust as needed.

The Essential Elements of a Business Plan

A thorough business strategy would normally contain the following critical elements:

Executive Summary: This is a brief explanation of your company's purpose, vision, and objectives, as well as the issue it will answer.

This part includes a full explanation of your company, including its history, unique selling proposition (USP), and the demand it meets.

Market Analysis: In this section, you will examine your target market, competitors, and industry trends. It is critical to completely grasp the industry into which you are venturing.

Describe your company's organizational structure, including its management team, important individuals, and their functions.

Items and Services: Describe the items or services your company will provide and how they will meet the demands of customers.

Marketing and Sales Strategy: Describe your marketing and sales plans, including how you intend to contact consumers, price, and distribution networks.

Financial predictions, such as income statements, cash flow estimates, and balance sheets, are included in this part.

Financing Requirements: If you're looking for outside financing, state how much you'll need and how you intend to utilize it.

Depart Strategy: Explain your long-term vision for the company, including how you want to depart, whether via a sale, merger, or other methods.

Business Planning Flexibility

While a business strategy is essential, it should not be seen as a strict blueprint. You should be prepared to adjust and revise your strategy when you obtain new insights and confront shifting market circumstances in the fast-paced world of business. Flexibility in your strategy will enable you to remain flexible and nimble, which is essential for startups.

Exploring Funding Options for Your Startup

Making your company vision a reality sometimes needs financial assistance. Entrepreneurs have many financing sources open to them, each with its own set of benefits and drawbacks. Let's look at some of the most prevalent startup financing sources:

1. Bootstrapping:

Bootstrapping is funding your firm with your own money and resources. It's a method to keep complete control of your enterprise while avoiding debt or handing up stock. It may, however, restrict your early development potential.

2. Family and friends:

You might solicit financial assistance from friends and relatives who believe in your company concept. This source is often more flexible than regular loans, but it has personal and emotional consequences.

3. Investors in the form of angels:

Individuals who donate funding to businesses in return for stock or convertible debt are known as angel investors. They often bring knowledge and useful contacts to the table. Angel investors may be an excellent source of early-stage investment.

4. Venture Capital (VC):

In return for stock, venture capital companies invest in businesses. They often contribute large funding, which may drive fast expansion. However, they often want a substantial part of ownership and power in return.

5. Crowdfunding:

Crowdfunding websites such as Kickstarter and Indiegogo enable you to raise cash from a huge number of individuals who believe in your idea. In exchange, supporters are often given gifts or early access to your product or service.

6. Loans for Small Businesses:

Small business loans from banks or internet lenders might help you get started. They often need interest-bearing payments, which might be a reasonable approach to finance your firm.

7. Grants:

Grants from government agencies or private groups may be available depending on the type of your firm. These are not repaid but may be quite competitive.

8. Incubators and accelerators:

In return for ownership or a part of your company, accelerator and incubator programs often give cash, coaching, and resources. These programs may help you guide your startup to success.

9. Strategic Alliances:

Collaboration with bigger firms or industry leaders may lead to financial assistance, access to resources, and possible market penetration. Strategic alliances might be an innovative method to finance your company.

10. Revenue Self-Funding:

You may finance your firm using money produced by early customers if your business plan supports it. This kind of development may give a self-sustaining strategy.

The best financing source for your company is determined by your business strategy, ambitions, and willingness to share ownership or return cash. It is critical to thoroughly consider your alternatives and their ramifications for your company's long-term success.

Key Considerations for Laying a Solid Foundation

The beginning period is also an excellent opportunity to set the groundwork for your company. Building a solid foundation entails many key steps:

Legal form: Select the right legal form for your company, whether it's a single proprietorship, partnership, LLC, or corporation. Each structure has taxes, liability, and governance issues.

Business Registration entails registering your company with the right government agencies. **This step assures that your company is legally recognized.**

Intellectual Property Protection: If your company depends on distinctive intellectual property, such as patents, trademarks, or copyrights, make sure it protects it against infringement.

Business Location: Determine whether you will run your company from a physical location, digitally, or a mix of the two. Consider cost, customer accessibility, and regulatory constraints.

Business Name & Branding: Select a distinctive and meaningful name for your company and develop a strong brand identity. This is critical for building recognition and trust.

Insurance: Evaluate your company's insurance requirements, such as liability insurance, property insurance, and worker's compensation. Insurance may protect your company from unanticipated risks.

Regulation Compliance: Understand and follow local, state, and federal rules. Tax obligations, licenses, permits, and industry-specific rules are all part of this.

Financial Systems: From the start, establish solid financial systems and accounting standards. This will assist you in efficiently managing your money and making educated choices.

Risk Management: Identify possible hazards to your firm and devise mitigation solutions. Long-term stability requires risk management.

Business Culture: Define your company's culture and values. This will assist you in making recruiting choices and foster a pleasant company environment.

Invest in the technology and infrastructure required to operate your organization effectively. This encompasses software, hardware, and communication devices.

The Methodology of the Lean Startup

The Lean Startup technique, created by Eric Ries, is one strategy that has gained traction in recent years. The Lean Startup methodology is distinguished by its emphasis on speed, adaptability, and verified learning. It is based on the following essential principles:

Build-Measure-Learn: The Lean Startup cycle is centered on developing a minimum viable product (MVP), analyzing its performance, and learning from data and user input. This iterative method allows you to constantly improve your product or service.

Validated Learning: The Lean Startup encourages entrepreneurs to verify their ideas and hypotheses via real-world experiments and consumer interactions, rather than generating assumptions.

Entrepreneurs are empowered to make educated choices based on the data and insights received through the Build-Measure-Learn cycle. They have the option of pivoting (making a substantial change in the product or strategy) or persevering (staying with the current method).

Accelerated Time to Market: The Lean Startup technique prioritizes speed and bringing your product or service to market as soon as possible. This enables you to test and iterate quickly.

Small Batch Manufacturing: Rather than investing in large-scale manufacturing, the Lean Startup promotes small-batch production to reduce waste and allow for changes based on consumer feedback.

Continuous Deployment: Lean Startup entrepreneurs strive to continually release changes and new features based on real-world data and customer demands.

Dropbox - A Lean Startup Success Story

Dropbox is an excellent example of a firm that successfully used the Lean firm technique. Drew Houston and Arash Ferdowsi, the creators, began with a simple idea: an easy-to-use file-sharing and storage service. They built an MVP (a simple file-sharing system), tracked its progress via user sign-ups, and learnt from consumer feedback.

Dropbox's iterative strategy allows it to constantly improve its offering. They utilized the knowledge they obtained to pivot or persist. They gradually added features based on verified learning. Dropbox is now a multibillion-dollar corporation, demonstrating the effectiveness of Lean Startup ideas in action.

Startup Phase Triumphs: Success Stories

To give more motivation, consider the following two business success stories that started with navigating the startup phase:

1st Success Story: Airbnb

Airbnb started as a small business created by Brian Chesky, Joe Gebbia, and Nathan Blecharczyk. To make ends meet, the founders leased out air mattresses from their residence. They rapidly understood that the idea might be turned into a profitable company. Airbnb established its platform, verified its strategy, and expanded to become a worldwide lodging powerhouse by starting small and employing the Lean Startup technique.

Success Story Number Two: WhatsApp

WhatsApp began as a basic chat software created by Brian Acton and Jan Koum. The creators' first goal was to establish a tool for keeping in contact with family members living in distant locations. WhatsApp swiftly gained popularity and expanded to become one of the most popular messaging applications in the world by concentrating on delivering a safe and ad-free texting experience. Later, Facebook paid $19 billion for WhatsApp, demonstrating the advantages of beginning small and establishing something that consumers actually love.

Progress in the Startup Phase

The starting period may be both exciting and challenging. It's a time for discovery, learning, and construction. Consider the following tips as you traverse this phase to ensure your success:

Maintain agility by embracing change and adapting to new knowledge. Prepare to pivot or endure in light of verified learning.

Client-Centric Approach: Concentrate on understanding and serving the demands of the client. Your most important resource is customer feedback.

Prioritize Resilience: Setbacks and challenges are unavoidable. Develop resilience to overcome obstacles and stay motivated.

Create a Strong Team: Surround yourself with people who share your vision and compliment your abilities. A strong team is essential throughout the initial period.

Financial prudence is the prudent management of one's resources. Spending should be modest and deliberate.

Embrace Technology: Use technology to increase efficiency and simplify procedures. Technology may be a valuable friend during the initial period.

Balance Vision with Pragmatism: While lofty dreams are important, don't lose sight of the practical actions necessary to fulfill them.

The startup phase is a voyage of discovery, and although it is plagued with difficulties, it is also a period of tremendous development and opportunity. Remember that every great entrepreneur has gone through this stage, conquering hurdles and uncertainty. Remember that the startup period is only a stepping stone to something bigger as you progress in your business path. You're well on your way to turning your concept into a healthy, profitable company with a great business plan, sensible finance alternatives, and a solid foundation.

Chapter 4: Building a Winning Team

"No entrepreneur succeeds alone." This straightforward reality is crucial to the entrepreneurial path. In Chapter 4, we'll look at how to put together a high-performing team. Building a winning team is sometimes the deciding factor between successful and unsuccessful projects. In this chapter, we'll look at how to find, inspire, and lead a group of people who share your vision and can help you achieve your company objectives. You'll learn effective tactics for team development and management, which will put you on the road to success.

The Influence of Collaboration

The notion of the lone genius building a corporate empire from the ground up is a rare exception in the world of entrepreneurship. Successful entrepreneurs often depend on the pooled skills, enthusiasm, and devotion of a team. There's a reason why the expression "teamwork makes the dream work." Here are some of the reasons why a winning team is essential:

Diverse Expertise: A team consists of people with a wide range of talents, backgrounds, and experiences. This variety may lead to more innovative ideas and more well-rounded decision-making.

Shared duties: Working in a team helps you to spread workload and duties, minimizing fatigue and ensuring that key activities get the attention they need.

Team members may inspire and support one another, helping to preserve morale during difficult times and enjoying victories together.

Leveraging abilities: A solid team enables you to capitalize on each member's abilities while compensating for their flaws. This increases both efficiency and efficacy.

Teams offer an atmosphere in which ideas may be argued, polished, and tested, resulting in creativity and adaptability.

Increased Productivity: Having more hands makes the task easier. You can do more in less time when you work as part of a team.

Now, let's look at how to put together a successful squad.

Finding the Right Team Members via Recruitment

Recruiting the ideal team members is an important first step in developing a successful team. The makeup of your team will have a significant impact on its performance and capacity to fulfill your company objectives. Here are some important factors to consider for effective recruitment:

Clearly Defined Roles: Before recruitment, clarify your team's roles and duties. Job descriptions that are well-stated will attract applicants who understand their anticipated contributions.

Cultural Fit: Consider not just prospective team members' abilities and credentials, but also their cultural fit with your company. It is critical to have shared values and be aligned with your corporate culture.

Individuals with the requisite abilities and skills for their responsibilities should be sought. Consider both hard and soft talents, such as communication and problem-solving.

Candidates with suitable experience and competence should be sought out. They should bring ideas and best practices to your company.

Passion and Motivation: People who are inspired by your goal and vision will be more devoted and dedicated to your company.

Teamwork and Collaboration: Assess a candidate's capacity to collaborate and adapt in a team context. A cohesive team is made up of people who can communicate and collaborate efficiently.

Adaptability is essential in the fast-paced world of business. Look for team members who are open to new experiences and learning.

Diversity: Make an effort to have a diverse staff. A diverse team may provide a variety of viewpoints and ideas, which can contribute to creativity and problem-solving.

The Interviewing Procedure

The interview procedure allows you to properly examine applicants. To conduct excellent interviews, consider the following strategies:

Structured Interviews: Create a structured interview procedure for each applicant, complete with a set of standardized questions. This facilitates comparison.

Behavioral Questions: Use behavioral questions to learn how former applicants handled various circumstances. This may provide information about their problem-solving and interpersonal abilities.

Consider skill exams or practical exercises to evaluate a candidate's skills, depending on the position.

Include questions on a candidate's alignment with your company's values and culture.

Reference Checks: Contact references supplied by applicants to learn more about their job history and personality.

Panel Interviews: Involving various team members in the interview process may give a variety of opinions while also ensuring a strong fit with the team.

Integration and Onboarding

Effective onboarding and integration are critical after you've found the right team members. Onboarding successfully sets the tone for an employee's experience and long-term performance. Here's how you should go about it:

Introduction: Provide a comprehensive introduction to new team members to acquaint them with the company's purpose, values, culture, and policies.

Training: Provide training on the tools, systems, and procedures that they will use in their responsibilities.

Mentorship: Assign a mentor or buddy to help new workers get started, answer questions, and provide assistance.

Schedule frequent check-ins and feedback meetings to address any problems, answer questions, and provide direction.

Cultural Integration: Encourage new workers to participate in team-building activities and events to assist them in integrating into the company's culture.

Clear Expectations: Make certain that new team members understand their roles, responsibilities, and performance expectations.

Leadership and Motivation

It is critical to motivate your team and provide excellent leadership to maximize their potential. Here are some methods for keeping your team motivated and engaged:

Inspire a Shared Vision: Share a compelling vision for your company that inspires passion and dedication among your team members.

Set Specific Objectives: Set specific, attainable objectives for your team that will offer direction and purpose. Divide long-term ambitions into smaller, more doable milestones.

Appreciation and recognition: Recognize and recognize your team's efforts and accomplishments. Morale and motivation are boosted by recognition.

Encourage team members to take ownership of their work and make choices within their areas of responsibility.

Regular Feedback: Provide constructive feedback and appreciation regularly. Feedback helps team members develop and feel appreciated.

Professional growth: Invest in the professional growth of your personnel. Employees are motivated by possibilities for advancement and training.

Fostering open, transparent communication is important. Encourage team members to discuss their thoughts and worries.

Lead by Example: Model the beliefs and behaviors you want your team to exhibit. Your leadership sets the tone for the culture of the company.

Resolution of Conflicts and Team Dynamics

Conflicts and problems are unavoidable in every team. An entrepreneur must be able to resolve conflicts effectively and manage team relations. Here's how to deal with these scenarios:

Proactive Conflict Resolution: Address disagreements and concerns as soon as possible to avoid them worsening. Encourage team members to talk freely and to settle disagreements productively.

Mediation: Act as a mediator when required to encourage talks and achieve resolutions.

Team Building Exercises: Plan team-building exercises and activities to develop team bonding and promote cooperation.

Inclusion and diversity: Foster an inclusive atmosphere in which all team members feel appreciated and valued. Encourage diversity while discouraging prejudice.

Implement feedback loops to evaluate team dynamics and find areas for development.

Chapter 5: Marketing and Branding Strategies

Any successful firm relies on effective marketing and branding initiatives. In this chapter, we'll look at how to create a compelling brand identity and a successful marketing plan. Understanding the concepts of good marketing and branding is critical whether you're establishing a new company or seeking to take your current one to the next level. You'll learn about the newest digital marketing trends and methods to help you reach your target audience and stand out in a crowded industry.

Marketing and Branding's Importance

Marketing and branding are critical components of establishing company success in the realm of entrepreneurship. These two parts are inextricably related and perform separate yet complementary functions:

Marketing is the employment of techniques and methods to promote and sell a product or service. It's the link between your company and your target audience. Effective marketing not only increases sales but also develops brand awareness and loyalty.

Branding, on the other hand, is the process of developing a unique and distinctive brand for your company. It incorporates your company's beliefs, purpose, and emotional connection with consumers. A good brand establishes confidence, distinguishes you from rivals, and aids in the growth of a devoted consumer base.

Marketing and branding are critical components of a successful company, and learning how to successfully harness them may have a huge influence on your entrepreneurial path. Let's look at how to create a captivating brand identity and a successful marketing plan.

Creating a Strong Brand Identity

Your brand identity is the public face of your company. It is your initial impression on clients and the enduring picture you leave in their thoughts. A strong brand identity fosters trust and an emotional connection with your target audience. The following are the essential factors to consider while developing your brand identity:

1. Establish Your Brand Values:

Begin by establishing the key values that your company represents. What causes do you support? What are the guiding principles in your choices and actions? Your values should be consistent with the beliefs and desires of your target audience.

2. Understand Your Audience:

Understanding your target demographic is essential for successful branding. You must understand their preferences, needs, and pain spots. Your brand identity should connect with your target audience and address their unique issues.

3. Develop a Remarkable Brand Name:

Choose a brand name that is memorable, distinct, and relevant to your company. A memorable name is a valuable asset in branding.

4. Create a Standout Logo:

A well-designed logo represents your business visually. It should be clear, straightforward, and immediately identifiable. Your logo will be shown on your website, business cards, goods, and other marketing tools.

5. Establish Your Brand Voice:

The tone and style of communication you utilize in all consumer interactions is referred to as your brand voice. It should be consistent with your brand's ideals and appealing to your target audience. Consistency is essential, whether it's friendly, professional, or hilarious.

Colors and imagery for the brand:

Choose a color palette and imagery that expresses the personality of your business and connects with your target audience. All branding items should utilize the same colors, typefaces, and graphics.

7. Create a One-of-a-Kind Brand Story:

A captivating brand narrative allows people to engage with your company on a more personal level. Your narrative should explain the roots of your company, its aim, and what makes it distinctive.

8. Maintain Consistency:

Brand consistency is essential. From your website and social media accounts to business cards and commercials, all marketing materials should convey a coherent picture of your company.

9. Increase trust and credibility:

Customers should have faith and confidence in your brand identity. Transparency, excellent goods or services, and regular delivery of commitments may all help to build confidence.

10. Adapt to the Times:

A powerful brand identity must be adaptive. To remain current and relevant in a dynamic marketplace, your branding may need to develop over time.

Marketing Strategies That Work

Once you've created a compelling brand identity, it's important to investigate efficient marketing tactics for reaching your target audience. Marketing is continually changing as a result of technical breakthroughs and shifting customer behavior. Consider the following great marketing strategies:

1. Content Promotion:

To attract and maintain a target audience, content marketing entails providing useful, informative, and entertaining material. This may include blog entries, articles, videos, infographics, and other types of content. Content marketing establishes your business as an expert in your sector and fosters trust among your target audience.

2. Marketing on Social Media:

Use social media tools to connect with your target demographic. Select the platforms where your target audience spends the most time. To establish a community around your company, provide compelling content, run targeted advertisements, and communicate with your fans.

3. Email Promotion:

Email marketing is still an effective method for reaching out to your target demographic. Create an email list and use it to send out updates, promotions, and useful stuff. Personalization and segmentation may help your email marketing perform better.

4. SEO (Search Engine Optimization):

Improve your presence in search results by optimizing your website and content for search engines. SEO is critical for growing organic traffic and your online visibility.

5. Social Media Marketing:

Collaborate with industry or specialized influencers to market your goods or services. Influencers have devoted followers who rely on their advice.

6. Paid Promotion:

Paid advertising, such as Google advertisements and social network advertisements, may assist you in swiftly reaching a wider audience. Effective ad campaigns should target certain groups and employ captivating ad language and imagery.

7. Video Promotion:

Video material is becoming more popular, and platforms such as YouTube are effective marketing tools. Make films that educate, amuse, or highlight your company's goods or services.

8. Networking and Collaboration:

Develop partnerships with other companies, leaders, and organizations in your field. Collaborations and partnerships may broaden your reach and promote your brand to new people.

9. Data Mining:

To acquire insights into your marketing activities, use data analytics tools. To improve your marketing efforts, analyze website traffic, social media engagement, and other important performance metrics.

Customer Feedback and Testimonials:

Encourage happy clients to submit feedback and testimonials. Positive feedback fosters confidence and credibility among prospective clients.

Trends in Digital Marketing

The digital marketing world is continuously changing, and keeping up to date on the newest trends may help your company gain a competitive advantage. Keep the following digital marketing trends in mind:

1. Individualization:

Customers today want individualized experiences. Data may be used to adapt marketing messages to individual tastes and habits.

2. Video Material:

The most engaging sort of material is video. Live streaming, short-form videos, and interactive material are all becoming more popular.

3. Optimization for Voice Search:

With the advent of speech-activated devices such as smart speakers and virtual assistants, it is becoming more crucial to optimize your content for voice search.

4. Chatbots and artificial intelligence:

Chatbots and artificial intelligence may improve customer service and automate monotonous processes, resulting in a better user experience.

5. Social Business:

E-commerce services are being integrated into social media platforms, enabling users to purchase straight from social postings and adverts.

6. Ethical and sustainable marketing:

Consumers are becoming more sensitive to environmental and ethical issues. In your marketing, emphasize your dedication to these ideals.

Nike - A Branding and Marketing Giant Case Study

Nike is an excellent example of a firm that has perfected the art of branding and marketing. The famous swoosh emblem and the tagline "Just Do It" are immediately identifiable. Nike has created a brand identity that is synonymous with athleticism, innovation, and quality.

Nike's marketing methods are centered on the emotional connection that exists between its brand and its consumers. Through its advertising campaigns, the company shares tales of success, inspiration, and resilience. It supports high-profile individuals and teams, emphasizing its link to sporting achievement.

Nike has efficiently used social media, content marketing, and influencer collaborations to interact with their audience in the digital age. Engaging films, strong narratives, and interactive experiences distinguish the brand's digital presence.

Nike has maintained its position as a worldwide leader in the sportswear business by combining a strong brand identity with creative marketing methods.

Brands That Achieved Success Through Marketing

Let's look at two success stories of firms that have succeeded at marketing:

Apple is the first success story.

Apple's marketing has been revolutionary in the technology business. In the late 1990s, the company's "Think Different" campaign challenged the existing quo and positioned Apple as a brand for creative and inventive people. Apple product introductions are events in and of themselves, bringing excitement and expectation. The firm constantly offers elegant and user-friendly goods, upholding the quality and innovation brand promise.

Coca-Cola Success Story No. 2

Coca-Cola's marketing has built an emotional connection with its customers. The brand is linked with joy and community. Coca-Cola's "Share a Coke" campaign, in which bottles were customized with people's names, promoted social sharing and became viral. Over the years, the company has also leveraged narrative and nostalgia to connect with its consumers.

Important Marketing and Branding Takeaways

As you begin your business path, keep the following marketing and branding tips in mind:

Create an Eye-Catching Brand Identity: Your brand's identity should represent your beliefs, connect with your target audience, and leave a lasting impression.

Understand Your Audience: Tailor your marketing and branding activities to connect with the tastes and demands of your target audience.

Stay Current: To remain competitive in the digital era, keep up with the newest marketing trends and technology.

Tell an Engaging Story: Storytelling is a strong marketing technique. Narratives may help you connect with your audience on a deeper level.

Measure and Adapt: Use data analytics to assess the performance of your marketing activities and make modifications as needed.

Be Consistent: Building trust and recognition requires consistency in branding and message.

Leverage New Technologies: To remain ahead in the digital marketing field, embrace upcoming technologies like artificial intelligence and voice search.

Make Ethical and Sustainable Practices a Priority: To match with the beliefs of current customers, emphasize your dedication to sustainability and ethical business practices in your marketing activities.

Inspire Emotion: Develop marketing initiatives that elicit emotion and connect with your target audience on a human level.

You may increase your company's exposure, interact with your target audience, and create a powerful and lasting brand by mastering the art of branding and marketing. These are priceless assets on your route to entrepreneurship success.

Chapter 6: Financial Management and Growth

In the fast-paced world of entrepreneurship, financial management is one of the most important cornerstones of long-term development and success. Chapter 6 is your all-inclusive guide to managing the complex world of financial management. This chapter is intended to provide you with the information and skills you need to manage your money efficiently, covering topics such as budgeting, cash flow management, and investing strategies. By the conclusion of this chapter, you will be well-versed in making educated financial choices that will support the long-term development and profitability of your firm.

Financial Management's Importance

Financial management is the foundation of every successful company. It includes the planning, arranging, and managing of a company's financial resources in order to fulfill its goals. Whether you are starting a new company or growing an existing one, efficient financial management is critical to attaining and maintaining development. Here are a few of the reasons why financial management is critical:

1. Decision-Making: Financial data serves as the foundation for sound decision-making. It assists you in making decisions that support your company's objectives and profitability.

2. Resource Allocation: Good financial management allows you to deploy resources properly, ensuring that your finances are spent where they are most required.

3. Risk Management: Knowing your financial status enables you to detect and manage possible risks, safeguarding your company from unanticipated obstacles.

4. Planning for expansion: Financial management allows you to prepare for expansion, whether it's extending your product line, entering new markets, or scaling your operations.

5. Financial Stability: Effective financial management contributes to your company's long-term financial stability and sustainability.

Budgeting is the cornerstone of financial management.

Budgeting is an essential part of financial management. It is the process of developing a financial strategy for your company. A well-structured budget acts as a road map for your financial activity, including your planned income and spending. Here's how to make a solid budget for your company:

1. Revenue Prediction:

Start by estimating your revenue. This entails calculating how much money your company will make in a certain time period. Your income projections should be based on a deep grasp of your market and clients.

2. Expense Calculation:

Identify and estimate all of your company's costs for the allotted time. This covers both fixed (rent, salary, and utilities) and variable (materials, marketing, and travel).

3. Cash Flow Administration:

Decide how you will handle your financial flow. Cash flow management is critical for ensuring that you have adequate money on hand to handle unexpected bills.

4. Budgeting Program:

Consider budgeting software or tools to help you simplify your budgeting process and simply monitor your financial success.

5. Constant Monitoring:

Monitor your budget vs actual performance on a regular basis. This allows you to keep on top of your financial situation and make changes as needed.

Management of Cash Flows

The control of cash flows is an important part of financial management. It all comes down to making sure your company has enough cash to satisfy its responsibilities while also allowing for growth and investment. Effective cash flow management entails the following steps:

1. Cash Flow Projection:

Estimate the money that will come into and out of your firm to forecast your cash flow. You may use this prediction to detect probable gaps and surpluses.

2. Management of Working Capital:

Make sure your company has enough operating cash to handle day-to-day needs. Working capital is defined as the difference between current assets (such as cash and accounts receivable) and current liabilities (such as accounts payable and short-term debt).

3. Credit Administration:

Effectively manage your trade credit. Negotiate good agreements with suppliers and urge clients to pay on time.

4. Inventory Management:

To minimize overstocking or stockouts, optimize your inventory levels. Excess inventory holds up cash, whilst insufficient inventory might result in lost sales.

5. Debt Administration:

If your company has debt, handle it wisely. Make sure your loan repayments are manageable and that you are not overwhelmed by interest payments.

6. Emergency Reserve Fund

Maintain an emergency reserve to meet unforeseen company expenditures or interruptions.

Investment Techniques

Investment is a major driver of corporate expansion. Your investments might take many different forms, such as increasing your product line, purchasing new equipment, or entering new markets. Consider the following investing strategies:

1. Investigation and Due Diligence:

Conduct rigorous study and due diligence before making any investment. Understand the investment's possible risks and returns.

2. Multiplication:

Spread the risk by diversifying your assets. Avoid committing all of your resources to a single investment, which may be dangerous if it fails to perform as predicted.

3. ROI (Return on Investment):

Any capital expenditure should be evaluated for its potential return on investment. Determine how long it will take to return your investment and begin earning a profit.

4. Long-Term Investments vs. Short-Term Investments:

Separate long-term and short-term investments. Long-term investments may include company expansion, whilst short-term investments may include the purchase of equipment or inventory.

5. Financing Alternatives:

Think about your funding choices. Will you utilize retained profits, get a loan, or seek outside investment? Each selection has an impact on your money management.

6. Check and Adjust:

Monitor the performance of your assets on a regular basis. Prepare to modify your investing tactics in response to the outcomes.

Financial Metrics and Ratios

Financial ratios and metrics give useful information about the financial health of your company. These figures may help you measure your company's performance, compare it to industry norms, and identify problem areas. Consider the following critical financial ratios and metrics:

1. Margin of Gross Profit:

The profitability of your main business is measured by this indicator. (Revenue - Cost of Goods Sold) / Revenue is how it's computed.

2. Gross Profit Margin:

The net profit margin measures your company's total profitability after all expenditures, including taxes and interest, have been deducted. Net Profit / Revenue is how it's computed.

3. ROI (Return on Investment):

ROI measures the return on a certain investment or expenditure. It is determined by dividing (Net Profit - Investment Cost) by the investment cost.

4. Present Ratio:

The current ratio evaluates the liquidity and capacity of your company to meet short-term commitments. Current Assets / Current Liabilities is how it's computed.

5th, the debt-to-equity ratio:

This ratio measures the financial leverage of your company. Total Debt / Total Equity is how it's computed.

6. Turnover of Accounts Receivable:

This score measures how fast your company collects past-due payments. Credit Sales / Average Accounts Receivable is how it's computed.

7. The Quick Ratio:

The fast ratio assesses your company's capacity to fulfill short-term obligations without the use of inventories. (Current Assets - Inventory) / Current Liabilities is how it's computed.

Cash Flow Coverage Ratio (CFCR):

This indicator evaluates your capacity to meet your debt commitments. Cash Flow from Operations / Total Debt Service is used to calculate it.

Financial Management Instruments

Various financial management tools and software may make managing your funds easier. Budgeting, accounting, invoicing, and financial analysis are common elements of these programs. Here are a few examples of popular financial management tools:

1. Microsoft QuickBooks:

QuickBooks is a well-known accounting program with tools for monitoring costs, issuing invoices, and managing accounts.

2. Xero:

Xero is another accounting software that offers options for invoicing, payroll, and spending monitoring to small companies.

(3) FreshBooks:

FreshBooks is accounting software for small companies that is hosted in the cloud. It makes billing, spending management, and financial reporting easier.

4. Mint:

Mint is a personal finance app that assists people and businesses in tracking costs, creating budgets, and monitoring their financial health.

5. Wave:

Wave provides small companies with free accounting, invoicing, and financial management software.

6. Accelerate:

Quicken is a personal financial application that helps users manage their accounts and assets.

Businesses That Have Mastered Financial Management

Let's look at two successful examples of companies that used good financial management to achieve exceptional growth:

Amazon's Success Story

Amazon's experience demonstrates the value of effective financial management. Because the firm initially prioritized long-term development above short-term profitability, it was able to spend extensively on infrastructure, technology, and logistics. While it lost money in the beginning, this approach eventually led to Amazon's supremacy in e-commerce and cloud computing. Today, Amazon maintains its position as one of the world's most valuable firms by reinvesting its revenues in growth projects.

Apple is the second success story.

Apple's financial management has been critical to its development and success. The firm has a strong financial sheet, which allows it to weather economic downturns and invest in R&D. Apple's strict approach to cash management, as well as smart acquisitions and investments, has resulted in continuous growth and innovation.

Key Financial Management and Growth Takeaways

Here are some critical things to consider about money management and development as you embark on your entrepreneurial journey:

Budgeting is the Foundation: Create a well-structured budget to successfully plan and monitor your financial actions.

Prioritize cash flow management to ensure you have enough liquidity to meet costs and invest in growth.

Strategic Investing entails assessing your investment options and diversifying to spread risk.

Financial Ratios and Metrics: Use financial ratios and metrics to measure the financial health and performance of your company.

Utilize Financial Management Tools: Investigate and employ financial management tools and software to streamline your financial duties.

Strategic Financial Management: Take a long-term perspective and invest in your company's development when it makes sense for your objectives.

Continuously Monitor and Adjust: Review your financial performance regularly and make modifications as required to promote growth.

Effective financial management is about making strategic choices that correspond with your company's objectives and vision, not simply statistics. When you master the art of financial management, you lay the route for long-term success and sustainable development. Your financial knowledge will be a valuable advantage on your entrepreneurial path, allowing you to manage the complicated financial environment and drive your company toward a bright future.

Chapter 7: Adapting to Change and Scaling

The corporate world is a dynamic, ever-changing environment in which adaptation is essential for long-term success. In Chapter 7, we set out to discover the secrets of expanding your company while being nimble and adaptable to change. Scaling your company entails developing it sustainably and smartly, while also being prepared to respond to changing market needs. We'll talk about tactics for growth, diversification, and staying ahead of the curve in an ever-changing industry.

The Importance of Adaptation to Change

In the corporate world, change is an unavoidable constant. Markets move, customer tastes change, and technology evolves. Adapting to these changes is not only necessary, but also a chance for progress. The inability to adapt and scale may lead to stagnation and, eventually, failure. Here are some of the reasons why adjusting to change is critical:

1. Market Dynamics: Consumer tastes, habits, and expectations are always changing. Businesses that adapt to these transformations will be able to benefit from new possibilities.

2. Market Competition: New firms join the market, while established rivals innovate. Adapting permits your company to remain competitive and relevant.

3. Technological Advances: Technology is progressing at an unparalleled rate. Adapting to new technology has the potential to increase productivity, create new income streams, and improve consumer experiences.

4. Economic Conditions: The economy may fluctuate, influencing consumer spending and corporate profitability. Adapting to economic changes is critical for survival.

5. Globalization: Global opportunities and risks might arise in a linked society. Adapting to a global market might open up new development opportunities.

Scaling Your Business Secrets

Scaling your company entails a planned and intentional expansion to gain profitability and market share. It is all about growing your business, client base, and income while preserving or even enhancing efficiency and effectiveness. Here are the keys to scaling success:

1. A well-defined vision and strategy:

Before you start growing, you should have a clear vision of where you want your firm to go. Create a growth plan outlining the actions and resources needed to attain your objective.

2. Processes That Can Be Scaled:

Make certain that your company procedures are scalable. This implies that if your company grows, your operations may expand without incurring substantial expenses or complexity.

3. Technology Investment:

Utilize technology to automate procedures, boost productivity, and enhance client experiences. Investing in the appropriate technology may be a growth driver.

4. Financial Planning:

Obtain the required financial resources for expansion. This might include getting funds, successfully managing financial flow, and distributing resources properly.

5. Recruiting Talent:

Create a skilled staff to help you develop. Hiring the appropriate people with the proper skills and expertise is critical to expanding effectively.

6. Customer-First Approach:

Maintain a laser-like concentration on your clients. Understand their changing requirements and preferences, and then change your goods and services to meet them.

7. Branding and marketing:

Increase the size of your marketing efforts to reach a larger audience. Make changes to your branding and message to appeal to new markets and client groups.

8. Broadening your horizons:

Consider expanding your product or service offerings to enter new markets or sectors. This may lower risk while also increasing income sources.

9. Strategic Alliances:

Form alliances with other companies to get access to new clients, distribution channels, or technology. Strategic partnerships may help businesses prosper.

10. Data-Informed Decision Making:

Use data analytics to guide your scaling efforts. Data may indicate market trends, client behavior, and areas that need development.

Scaling and Adaptation Strategies

Scaling is not a one-size-fits-all procedure; it is determined by your company's specific circumstances, industry, and ambitions. Consider the following tactics for scaling and adapting to change:

1. Organic Development:

Organic growth is the process of increasing your firm from the inside. It might mean expanding your product line, entering new markets, or servicing new consumer groups. To finance growth, this technique often depends on retained profits.

2. Strategic Partnerships:

Establish strategic alliances or collaborations with other companies in your field. This might result in the creation of new distribution channels, access to new markets, and the sharing of resources or knowledge.

3. Commercialization:

Consider franchising your successful company concept to others. This may lead to quick growth without having to bear all of the risks and expenditures alone.

4. Acquisitions and mergers:

Investigate the potential of purchasing or merging with other companies. This allows you immediate access to new markets, technology, or consumer bases.

5. Internet Presence:

Use the internet's capacity to broaden your reach. An online presence may help you get access to a worldwide market and communicate with clients around the clock.

6. Licenses:

Licensing your goods or services to other firms allows you to enter new markets or sectors without having to have a physical presence.

7. Exportation:

Consider exporting if you have things that can be marketed globally. This may be a deliberate approach to expanding into new areas and diversifying your consumer base.

8. Product Versatility:

Increase your product or service options to better meet the demands of your customers. This may help you enter new markets and increase your income.

9. E-commerce and mobile apps:

Invest in mobile applications or e-commerce platforms to make your items or services more accessible. The mobile market is constantly expanding.

10. Research and Innovation:

Invest in R&D to keep ahead of market trends and create novel goods or services that set businesses apart.

Airbnb Case Study: Scaling and Adapting to Market Changes

Airbnb is a shining example of a company that has mastered the art of expanding and responding to market shifts. Airbnb, which was founded in 2008 as an online platform for renting lodgings, upended the conventional hotel sector. Its business strategy allows homeowners to rent out their homes, giving passengers additional options at frequently reduced pricing.

As it grew quickly, Airbnb faced several problems, including regulatory concerns, competition, and the need to adapt to changing visitor tastes. To solve these issues, Airbnb expanded its offerings to include activities, restaurants, and boutique hotels. In addition, the firm invested in technology to improve the client experience and safety precautions.

During the COVID-19 epidemic, when the tourism industry was confronted with unprecedented obstacles, Airbnb displayed adaptation by providing new services such as Online Experiences to appeal to a distant and stay-at-home audience. Airbnb has thrived and innovated by being adaptable and sensitive to market developments.

Zoom's Success Story: Adapting and Scaling

Zoom Video Communications is yet another remarkable success story of market flexibility and expansion. Zoom was founded in 2011 to deliver video conferencing for corporate applications. While it grew in popularity, its ultimate breakthrough occurred during the COVID-19 pandemic in 2020, when remote work and online communication became the norm.

Zoom quickly adjusted to this change in demand, making its platform more accessible to a wider audience. It provided free personal versions and incorporated tools to improve virtual meetings and events. Zoom's user base skyrocketed as a consequence, and the firm saw extraordinary growth. It was able to swiftly increase its operations while maintaining the quality and security of its services.

Key Takeaways for Scaling and Adapting to Change

As you negotiate the ever-changing world of entrepreneurship, keep the following crucial points in mind for adjusting to change and scaling:

Change Is Unavoidable: Accept change as an opportunity for progress rather than a challenge to conquer.

Scaling necessitates strategy: Create a clear scaling plan that is in line with your company's vision and objectives.

Maintain Customer Focus: Constantly understand and react to your consumers' wants and preferences.

When Appropriate, diversify: Consider diversification to decrease risk and increase income sources.

Be Responsive and Agile: Respond quickly to market changes and developing opportunities.

Use Technology to Simplify Operations, Improve Customer Experiences, and Expand Your Online Presence.

Strategic Partnerships: Work with other companies to get access to new markets, consumers, and resources.

Innovation is essential: Invest in Ramped to remain ahead of market developments and client expectations.

Maintain Quality: Make certain that your scaling efforts do not degrade the quality of your goods or services.

Continuous Monitoring entails regularly assessing your company's performance and adapting as required.

Scaling your company and adjusting to change are not one-time events; they are a constant process. It needs a combination of vision, strategy, creativity, and a willingness to adapt. When done correctly, it may lead to significant development and long-term success. Your capacity to grow and adapt is an important advantage on your entrepreneurial journey, allowing you to succeed in the face of changing markets and client requirements.